Family

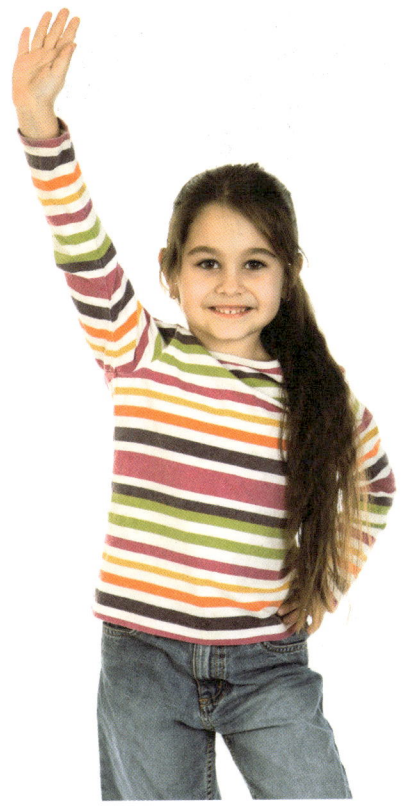

Seed Learning

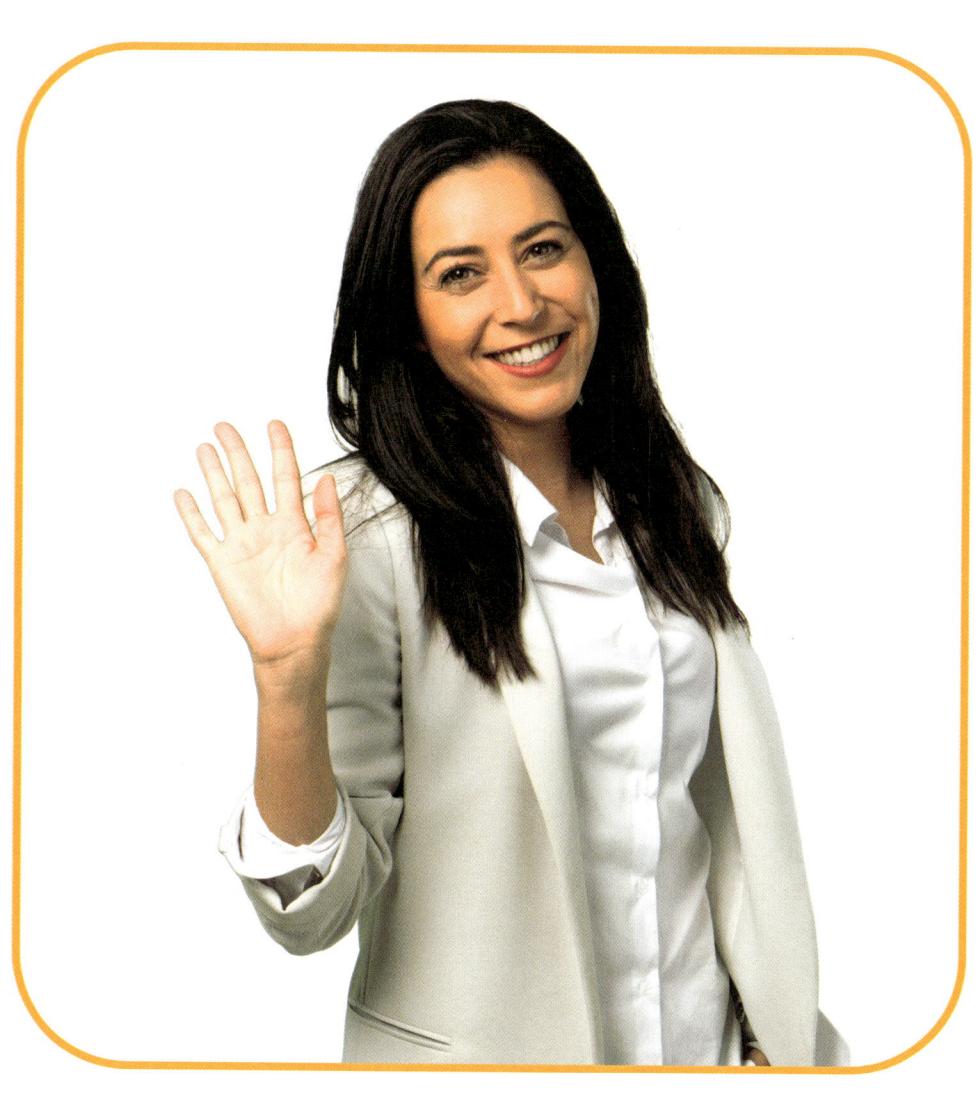

mom

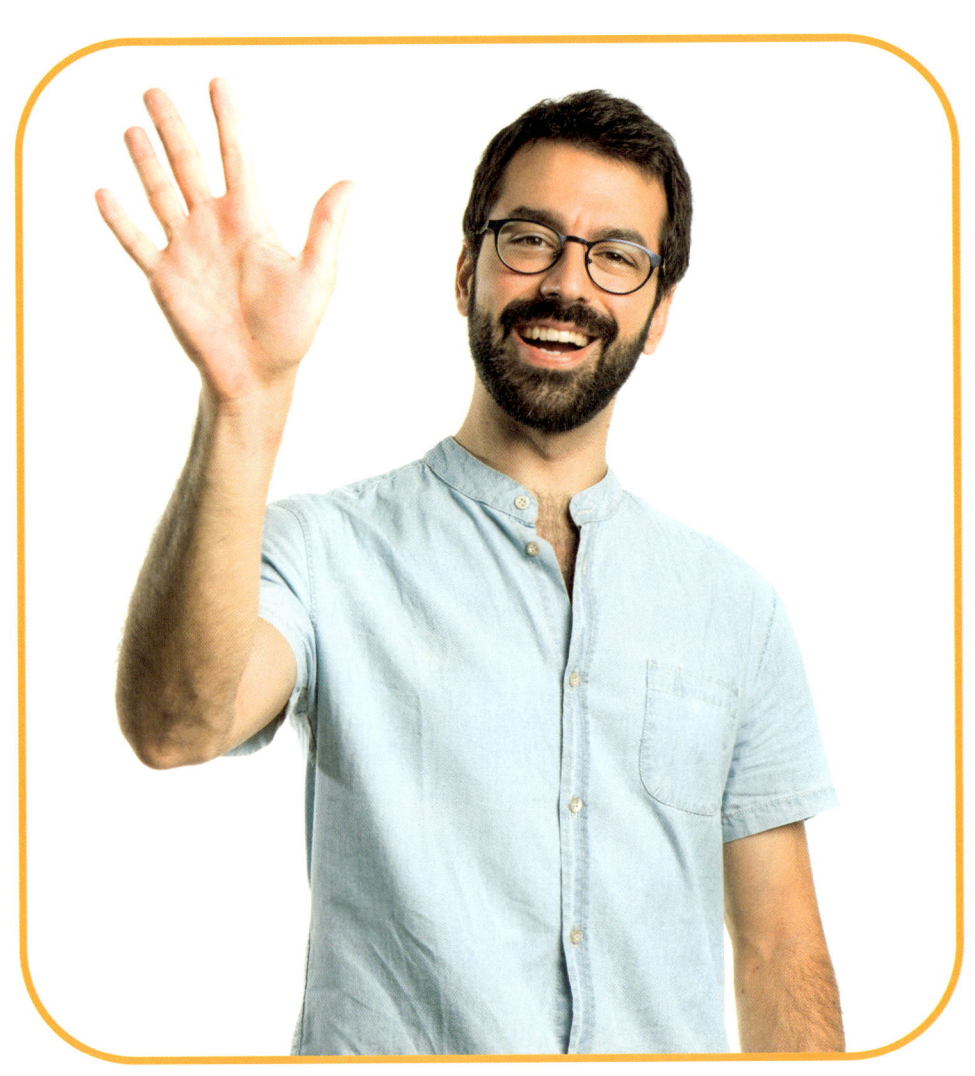

dad

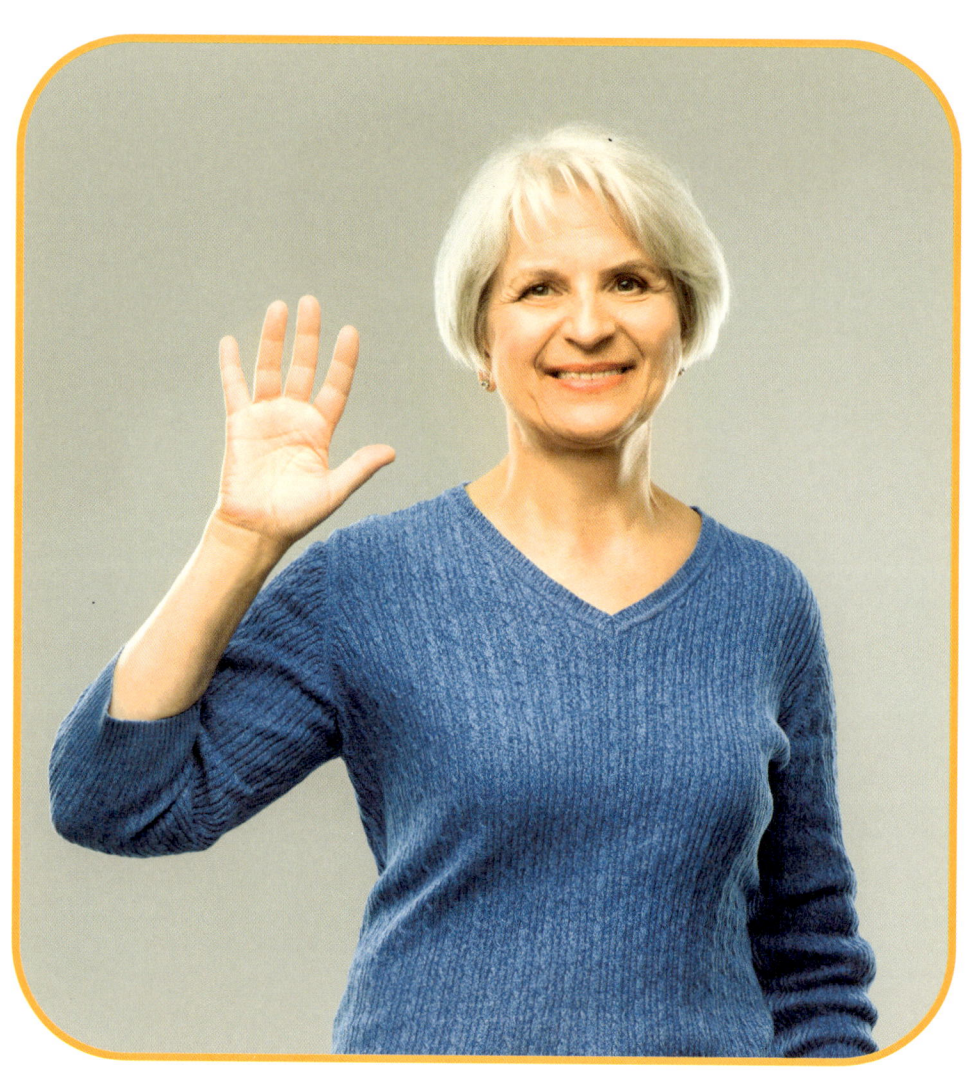

grandma

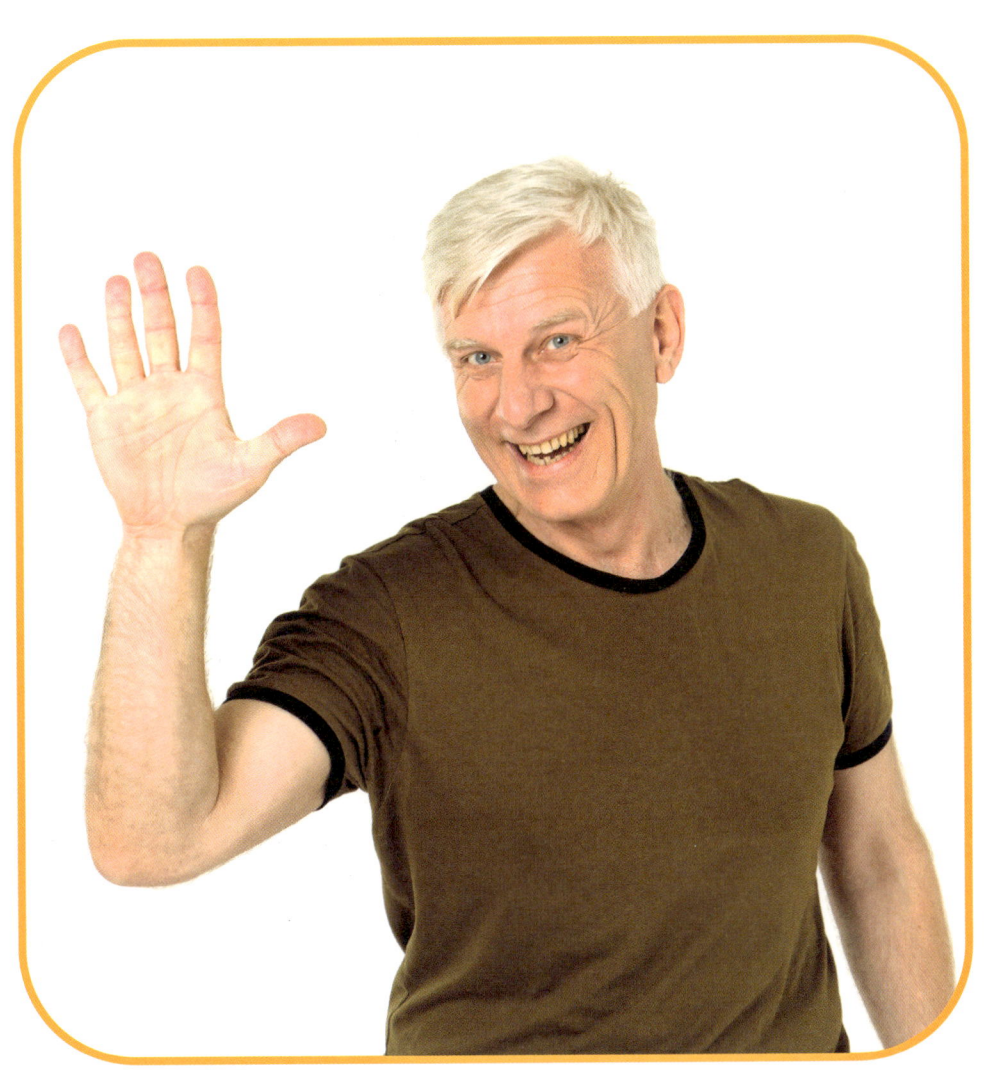

grandpa

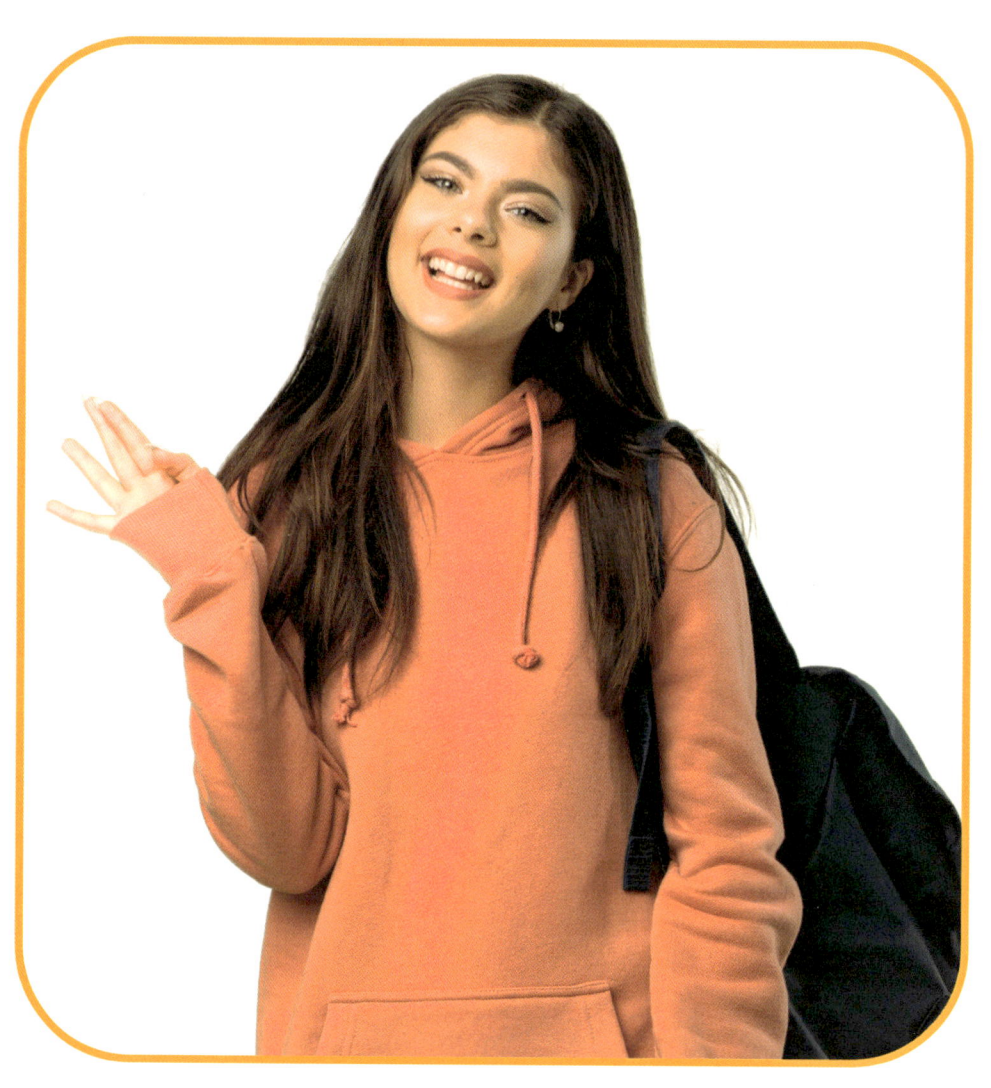

sister

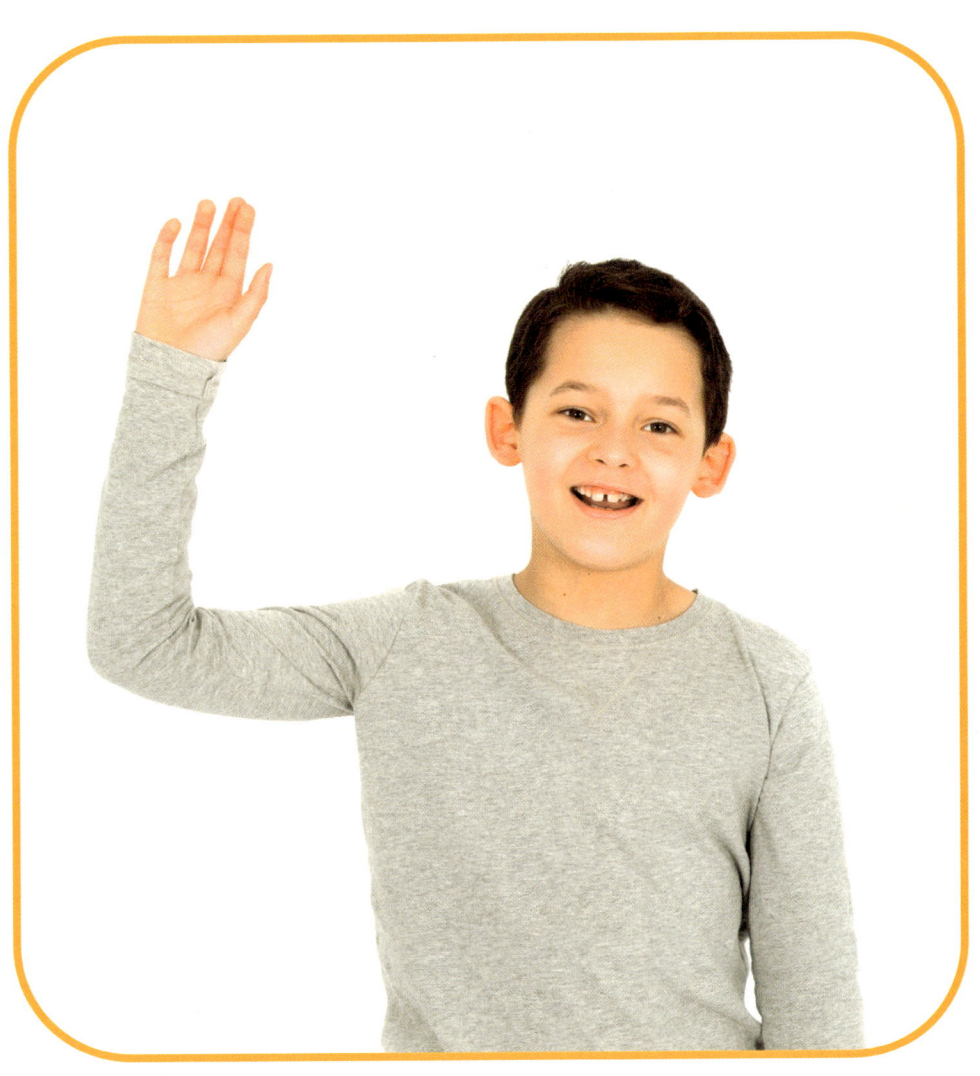

brother

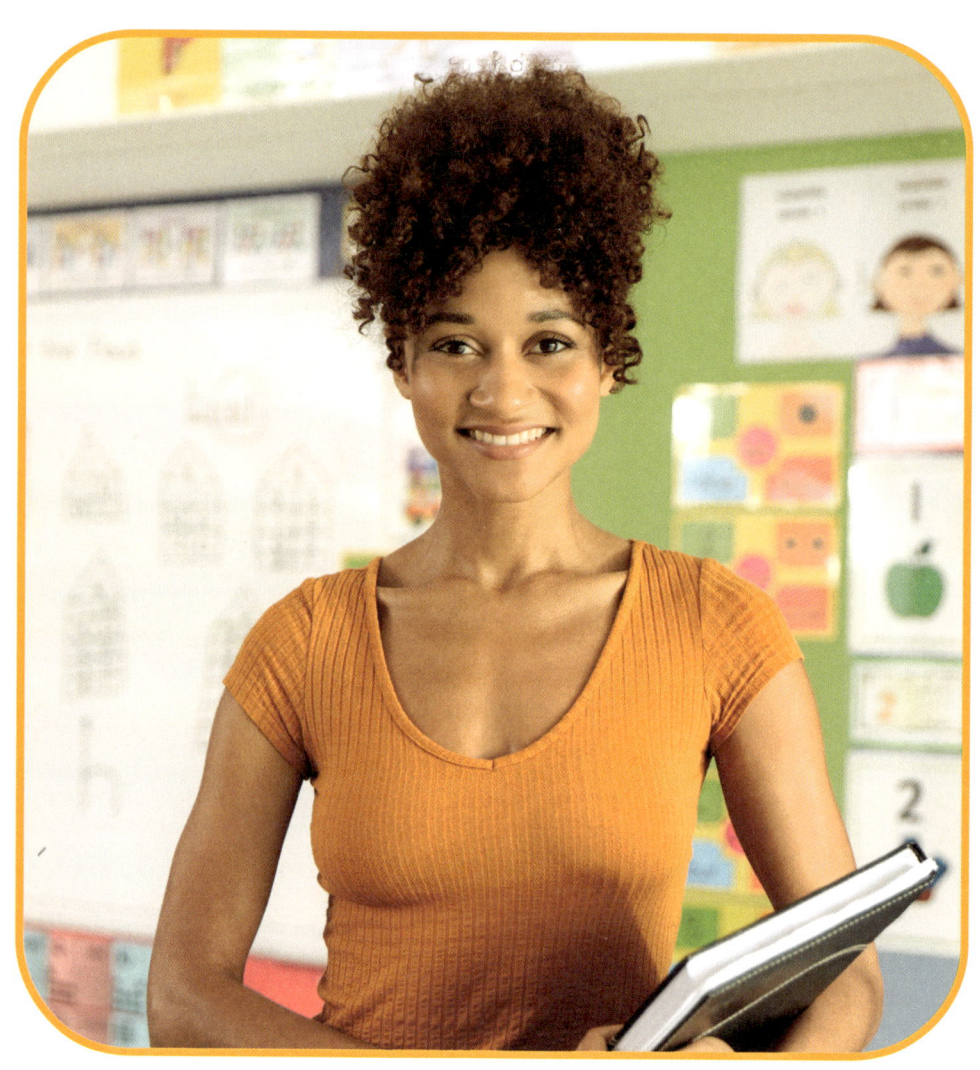

teacher

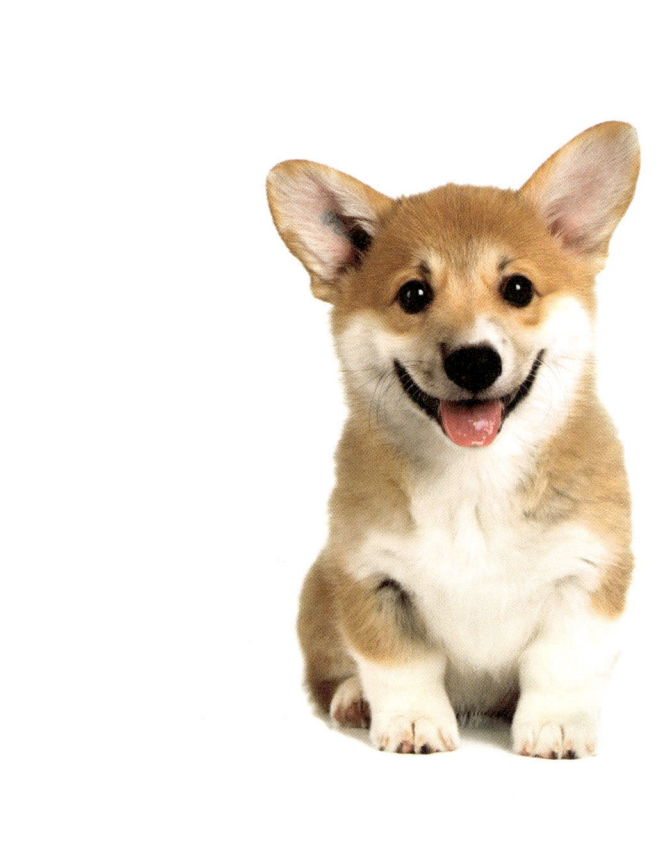

puppy

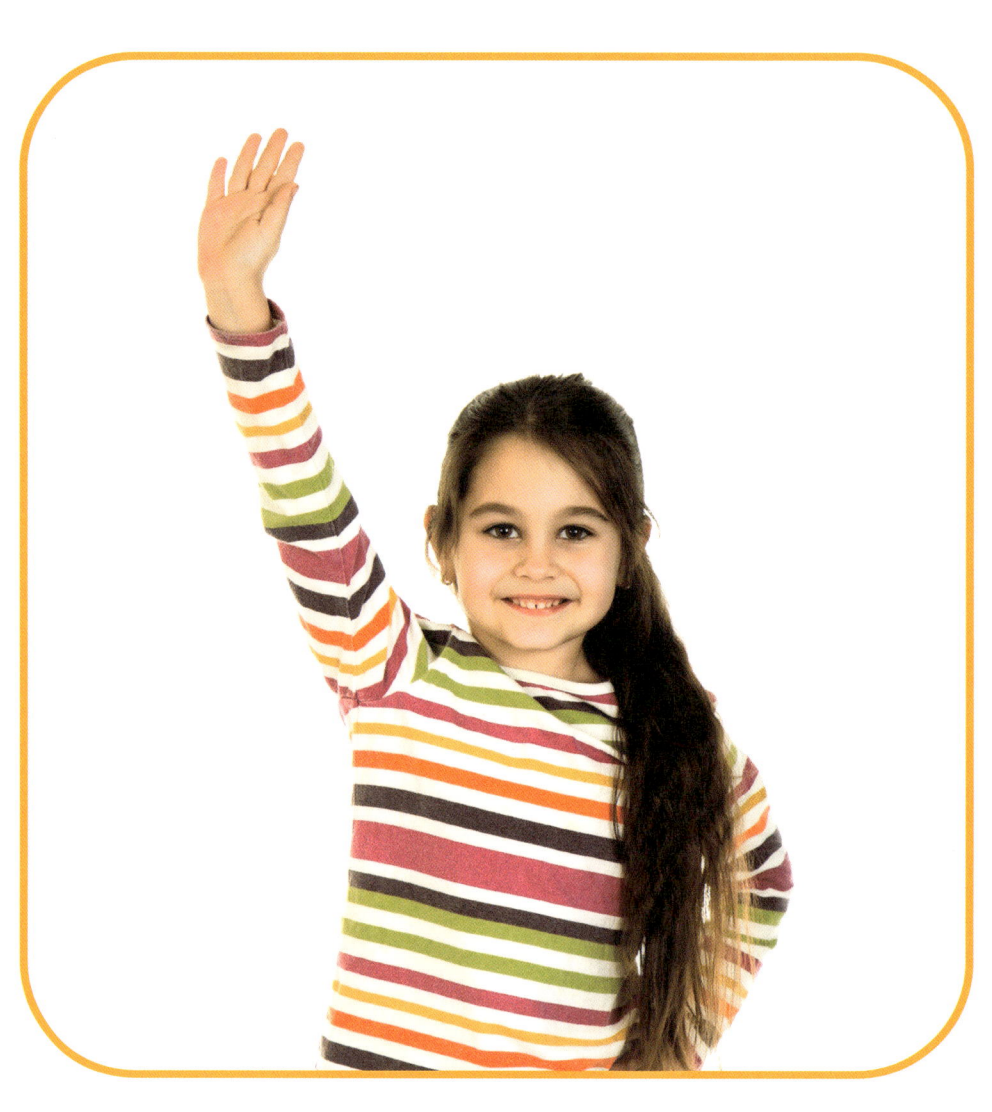

Hi, Mom.

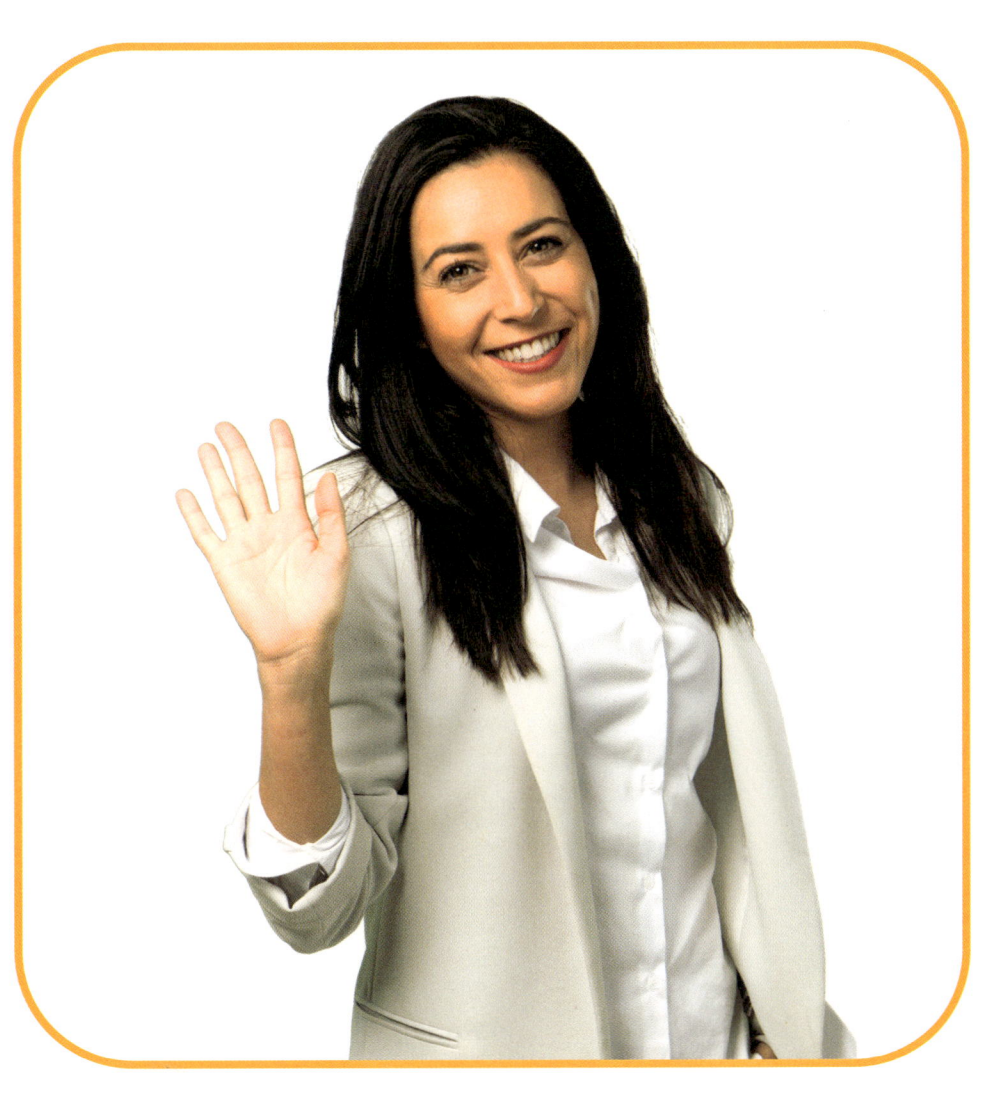

Hi.

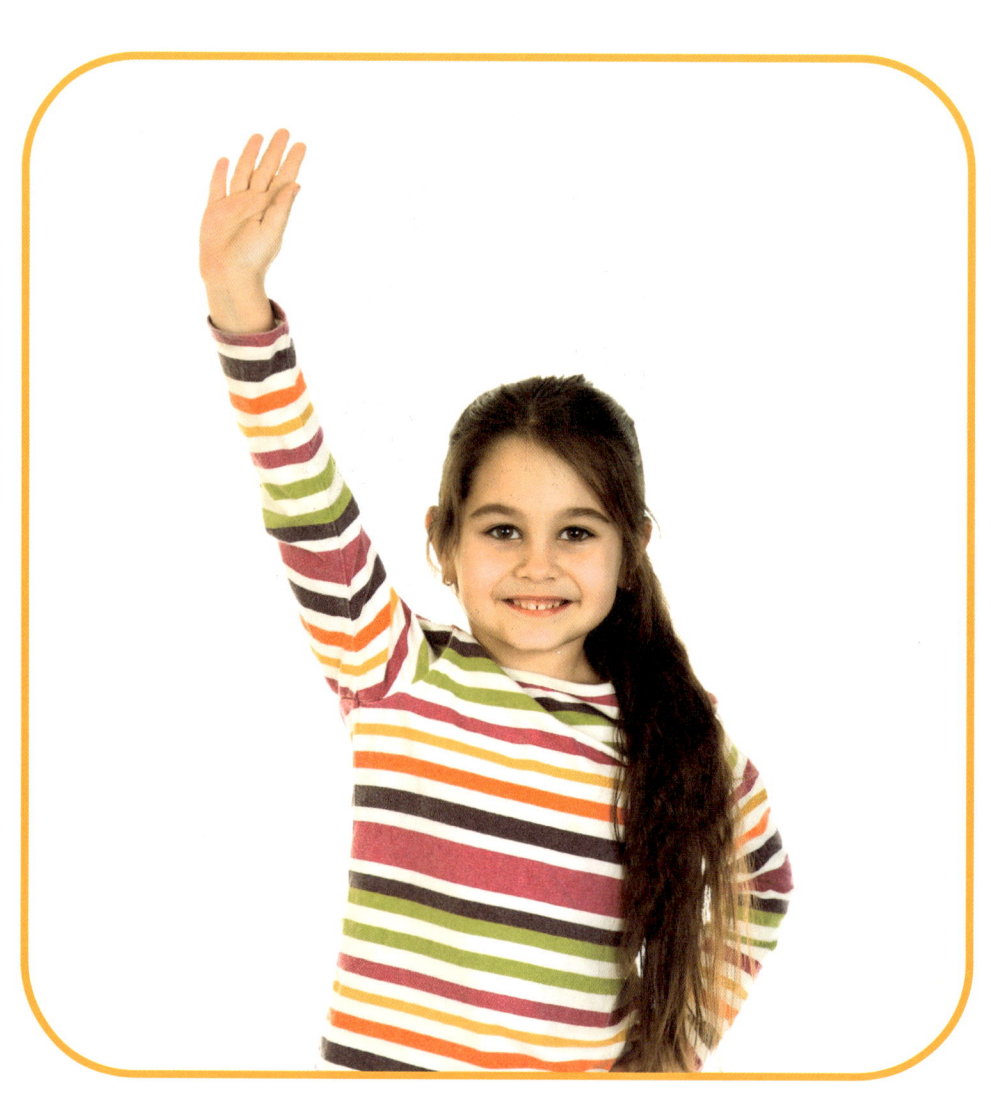

Hi, Dad.

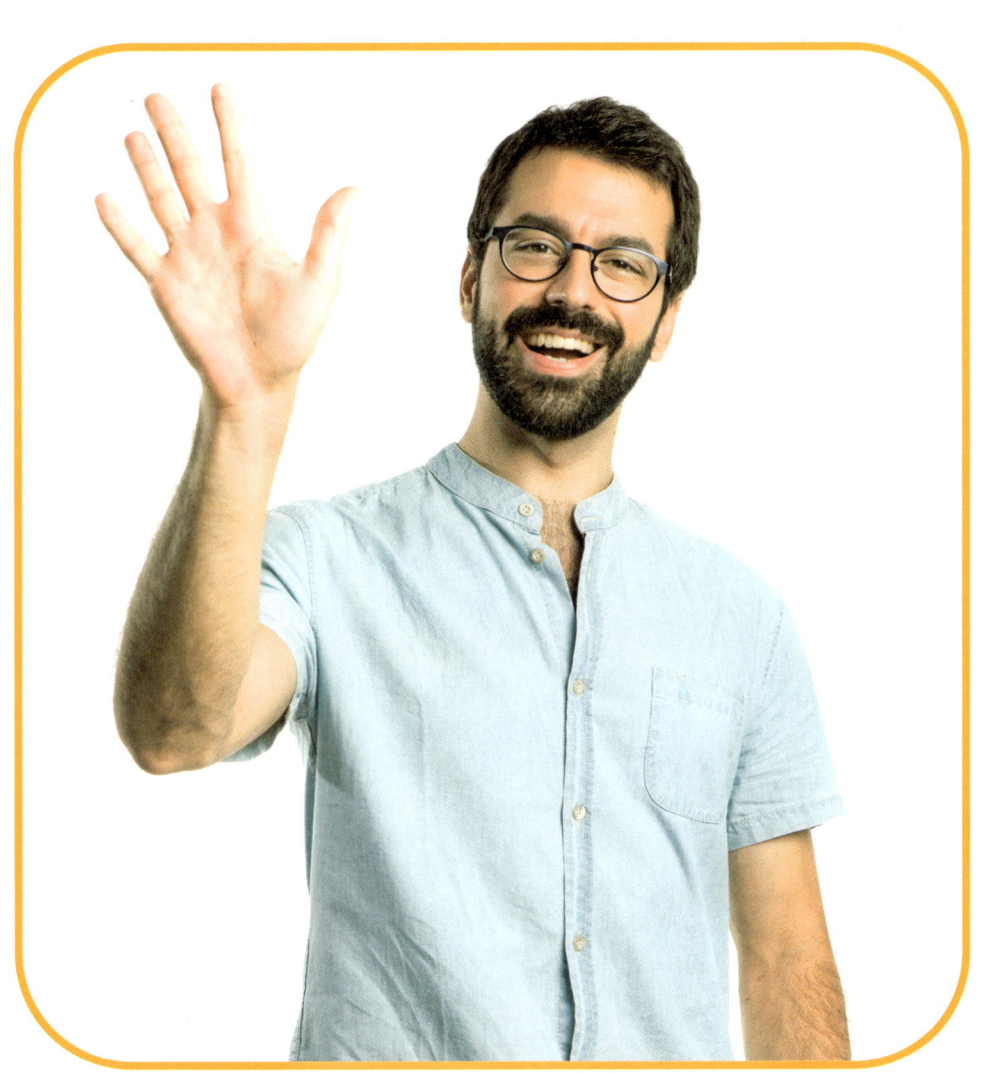

Hi.

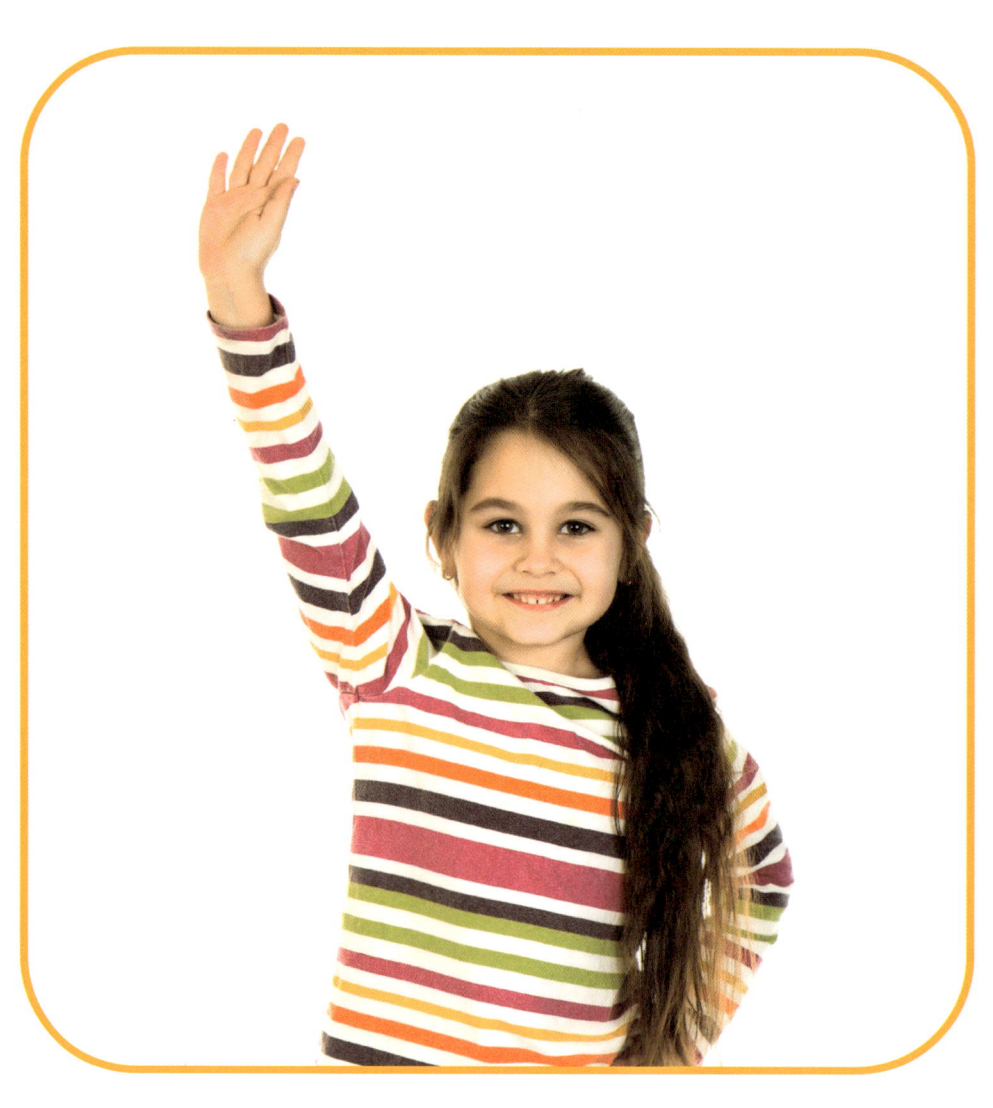

Hi, Puppy.

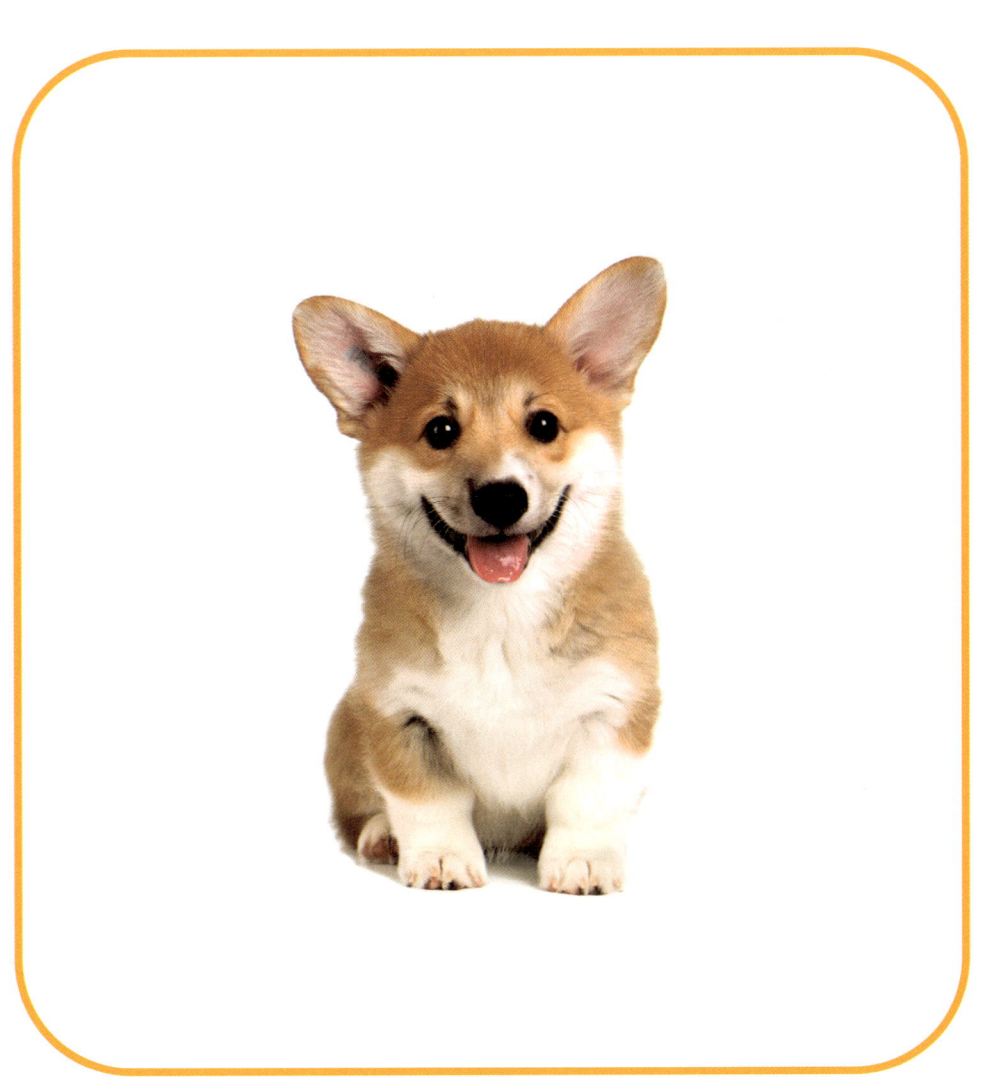

Woof.

Word List

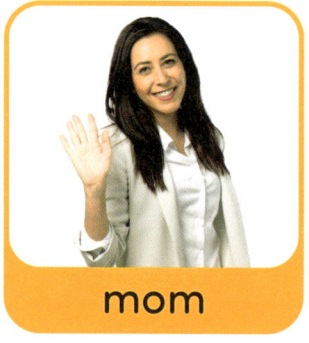
mom

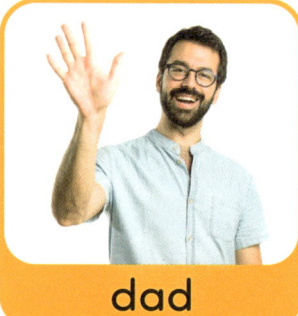
dad

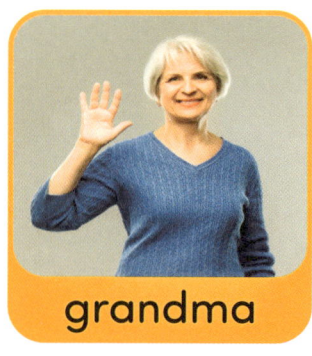
grandma

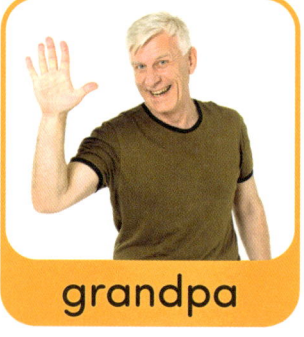
grandpa

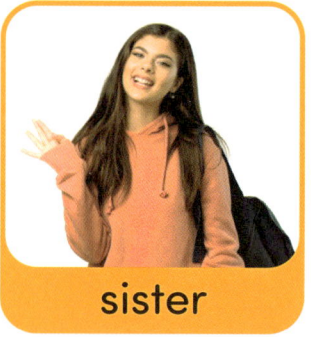
sister

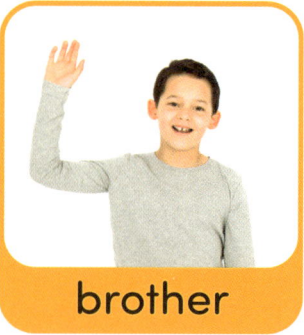
brother

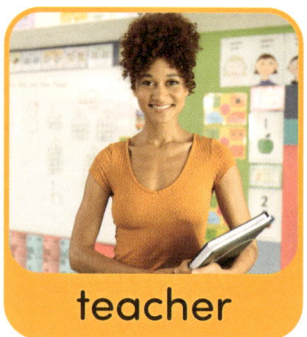
teacher

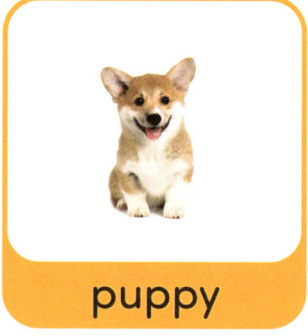
puppy